OPTIMAL CHILD DEVELOPMENT: 100 TIPS FOR PARENTS

DR DHEERAJ MEHROTRA

Contents

Preface

Optimal Child Development: 100 Tips For Parents is a work which defines and engages parents about How do parents encourage their children to grow up with a genuine sense of who they are, a solid set of values, and the self-assurance to express their creativity?

A result-oriented work is all set to engage the parents and work wonders. This book will serve as an invaluable reference and guide for youngsters to develop a healthy sense of self and the resilience to overcome obstacles in their lives.

Happy Learning!

www.authordheerajmehrotra.com

ONE
OPTIMAL CHILD DEVELOPMENT

Naturalistic Intelligence Among School Kids

**Dr Dheeraj Mehrotra,
Principal, Kunwar's Global
School, Lucknow, India**

We understand natural intelligence as the ability to appreciate, categorise, classify, explain, and connect the things of everyday life with nature. One of the forms of intelligence that manifests itself early on in a person's life is naturalistic intelligence. There is a connection between the activities that have been outlined and natural intelligence. One may argue that each newborn has specific innate intelligence from birth. They make incremental environmental improvements by investigating the planet's flora and animals to better it. The naturalistic intelligence category is one of the eight intelligence subcategories included in Howard Gardner's theory of multiple intelligences, which he suggested. Gardner defines intelligence as "the capacity to solve problems or develop goods relevant to a particular cultural context or community." It is essential to remember that intelligence is "the capacity to solve problems or develop goods that are relevant in a particular cultural context or community."

Understanding Gardner's Take on Naturalistic Intelligence?

According to Gardner, natural intelligence is the capacity to recognise, classify, and exert influence over everything in one's environment, including animals, plants, and objects. Naturalist intelligence may sometimes be coaxed out of students via classroom activities. Creating habitats, taking care of animals and plants, and gathering and arranging things like rocks, insects, and snails into groups are some examples of habitat creation and maintenance. We are distinct from other animals in that our innate behaviours do not entirely control us; instead, we perceive ourselves as different from the natural environment. It would seem that the great majority of other creatures do not even have the potential to depart from the behaviours dictated by their instincts.

A broad spectrum can be used to describe the degree of connection that diverse societies and people all around the globe have with their natural environments. For instance, there is a significant variation in the degree to which individuals in India are tuned into the natural rhythms and cycles. There are nine different forms of intelligence, and one of the most basic types is naturalist intelligence, by the notion of multiple intelligences.

People who have developed a naturalistic intelligence are recognisable by the fact that they take pride in their gardens and have a strong interest in flora. They like spending time at home tending to the many plants there. They watch out for them and conduct constant checks to ensure that their lives are complete and that nothing is lacking. As defined by Howard Gardner, naturalist intelligence is the capacity to identify differences in natural settings, such as distinguishing one species of plantain from another or recognising one cloud pattern from another.

How might educators include students in putting natural intelligence into practice?

Have a good time in the fresh air by participating in outdoor pursuits like hiking and camping. They take pleasure in day trips to rural areas, such as farms and fields. They make hiking and camping a regular part of their routine or entertainment. Howard Gardner identified naturalist intelligence as one of the nine distinct forms of intelligence. The degree to which a person is sensitive to nature and the world around them is directly related to their level of intellect. People skilled in this intelligence often like tending gardens, caring for animals, or researching plants or animals. Gardner believes that zookeepers, biologists, gardeners, and veterinarians are examples of persons who have high levels of naturalist intelligence.

As responsible parents, we must ensure that our students learn how to deal with the ups and downs of life. Allow children a certain amount of independence to develop academically, socially, emotionally, and physically.

The United Nations Educational, Scientific, and Cultural Organization (UNESCO) discusses the happy schools' framework, which includes People, Processes, and places. The symbolic analysis found under People relates to the friendships and relationships that exist within the school community, the positive teacher attitudes and attributes, the respect for diversity and differences, the positive and collaborative values and practises, the teaching working conditions and well-being, as well as the teacher's skills and competencies.

ᕤᕤᕤ

UNESCO is doing more research on the Process, which examines topics such as the manageable and equitable workload, the spirit of cooperation and collaboration, as well as teaching and learning methods that are exciting and interesting.

The following are some of the optimal child development tips for parents:

Believe in Parenting Power! Parenthood is a gift. Stay Strong! Good parenting causes headaches, bad parenting causes heartaches.

Prepare for the most challenging task Parenting is your most demanding job or will be. Learn the ropes. Be flexible.

ᗰᗰᗰ

Learn "infant care" Pregnancy starts with parenting. You must cease smoking and drinking while pregnant. Tea and coffee are off-limits. You must eat well, relax, etc. First-time parents may learn a lot from seasoned parents. Parents teach you a lot.

Stop moaning If your youngster doesn't follow you, don't whine. Complaining hurts your child's ego. A good parent loves their kid for who they are. Keep your expectations high by increasing your child's confidence. Good parents let their kids be responsible.

▷▷▷

Encourage appropriate risks. Encourage your youngster to take modest risks for personal growth. Our kids are equals, not servants. Don't respond hastily to your child's blunders. Before reacting, analyse the circumstance. Always love your kid. Everyone makes errors and always will.

Give your kids power. Don't make things easy for your child; effort is key to success.

Be honest with your kid. Don't sugarcoat the truth if your kid tests you with a tantrum, rage, weeping, or rudeness. Leave and tell him to discuss it later. Don't ignore your child when he wants to talk. Listen carefully. Don't interrupt; speak after he ends. Kindly firm! Don't wait for your youngster to initiate a conversation. Encourage him to ask questions. "Don't compare me to other kids; it makes me envious." Always be communicative; never discontinue your child's call. Communication helps you and your kid communicate. Show good judgement: Teach morality. Make them do the right thing.

Never withhold affection to inspire your kid.

Follow your rules. How can your kid obey the rules if you don't? Never yield to cries, demands, or sulking. Be a role model: If you want a lovely child, be one. Always be good in front of the kids. If you display severe emotions (anger, disappointments, etc.) in front of your kid, he or she may emulate you (believe me, children are good at imitating). Humans learn via imitation; it's the first approach. Imitate skilful people.

Children aren't adept at decoding words. They don't care about "I love you" Hugs, kisses, and presents show your affection. Positive parents raise optimistic children. Don't blame your shortcomings. Parents: "Correct my faults instead of shouting" If you're negative, your kid may be too. Your kid won't adopt negativity if you're positive. Your youngster should feel comfortable with you.

You must reassure them. Feel secure with your kid. If you want your kid to trust you, create trust. Don't tell anybody his secret, not even your spouse. Reflect on your upbringing to improve your parenting. Implement your favourite ideas. Avoid terrible experiences.

Share your life experience: Your youngster may learn a lot from you. Tell your kids how you did things, behaved, and grew through time. Finding time for yourself doesn't imply you don't care about being a good parent. Happy parents can raise happy children. Don't spank: Your youngster will grow aggressive if spanked. Parents: "Encourage me to do my homework."

No threats. "I hate studying" Read to your child: Kid psychology helps you understand your child. Analyze your child's feelings and thoughts. Honour his views. Read parenting books and use what you've learned. There's a lot of research on parenting. Parents: "Your trust in me gives me a lot of bravery."

Talk to other parents. They'll offer valuable advice. Mom & Dad: "Give me household duties to perform." I learn life skills." There are a lot of various ways to achieve success. Encourage children to look for chances to participate in constructive activities whenever they can. To be charitable, to make a positive contribution to one's community and the well-being of society as a whole, and to help others in some manner.

Let them be: Encourage your kid to be themselves. Help them be Shashank, not Ravi. Understanding your privilege as a parent is a secret. The kid came to make you happy, not hurt you.

Don't make them behave like adults: Children grow up. Normal. Don't expect your youngster to behave like an adult. Why would you expect an adult to act like a child? Life is unpredictable. Therefore, it teaches survival skills. Prepare your youngster for numerous situations like earthquakes, strangers, and more.

You're brighter than your youngster, but he's not stupid. Let him learn. Let him study independently. Learning increases income.

Nurture your child's innate spirituality by letting him learn from his environment. Do you enjoy messing with your business? Nope. Don't interfere with a child's world. Do you want your kid to be afraid? Create a child-friendly environment. Letting him do what he wants doesn't imply he can always do wrong.

Let a youngster be free: You should govern your kids since you're his parent and won't damage them. Overcontrolling is terrible. True love isn't giving your kid everything they want or showering them with kisses.

True love involves doing his best. If you're strict with your kid, he won't trust you and may despise you. Never compare kids. Every child's creativity.

Teach youngsters about taxes! 30% of their ice cream. "When I'm having a tantrum, all I need is a hug," said the child.

Don't micromanage: Sit underneath the youngster and attempt to grasp his thinking.

Be attractive: Your youngster will like you if you entice him. He'll follow if he likes you. If you want to be loved, offer love. Your kid will return your pet. Respect is a two-way street, much like love.

Your kid will respect you if you appreciate them. Spend precious time understanding your kid. Spending time with your kid will build a friendship. Parenting may be difficult. When anxious, you may be rude to the youngster. Don't take out your stress on your kid. Most people can't escape the anger, but you must manage it around your kid. If you can't stop banging on the door, your kid will too.

A good parent is someone who has a healthy connection with their spouse. If you have a healthy marriage, your kid will thrive. The youngster is little but has a personality and character. You want your kid to be the greatest, but does he want to do what you want? Encourage self-reliance.

Allow them to develop their interests and talents. Do not expect your youngster to pick up his textbook while the TV is on. You need money for a proper school, upbringing, and medical expenditures. Invest in your child's future by saving money. Make punishment the final resort in behavioural control. Punishment should only be employed when other options fail.

Research on parenting and child psychology shows that punishment is sometimes essential to discipline, enforce norms, and foster learning. Children might be picky eaters, so encourage them to consume healthful meals.

Sleep early and rise early to maintain a healthy lifestyle. Don't party too much or stay out late. Your youngster watches you closely. Teach your youngster the significance of exercise by jogging or cycling with him. We live in a multicultural world; teach tolerance. Teach your youngster about different cultures. Encourage your youngster to engage in spiritual or religious activities, but don't push it.

Watch your child's school, after-school, and community activities. Know your child's pals and their parents. Your child's pal might reveal a lot about him. Protect your youngster from danger. Swings may be harmful. Protect your youngster.

Don't let the youngster direct you. You can't go back once you play by his rules out of love. Show the youngster who's boss. Set a barrier so your youngster may pursue his interest in a secure atmosphere. Your youngster has self-esteem; don't damage it. You don't want somebody to harm your self-respect, do you? If your kid wants to tie his shoelace, wear his shirt, etc., let him. This is also healthy. Never fix everything. Let your youngster decide. Don't interfere till he quits.

You teach self-reliance and resilience by letting the youngster discover his answers. Discipline your child: Discipline starts from home. Standardize what's permitted and not allowed. Discipline isn't about constraint. Discipline your kid. Discipline isn't restraining them. Disciplining involves letting them act well so they can be good. Children are naturally destructive; they like tossing and smashing things. Early prevention is key. Don't establish too many rules.

Too many restrictions overwhelm children. Tech-Candy Time should come after study, play, and supper. If you're harsh to your kids, they'll *be rude to you. They will mimic your rudeness. Children will mimic your rudeness. Children understand politeness. They may initially follow you if you're disrespectful, but they'll revolt afterwards.*

Know your child's age and act appropriately. Baby and toddler care are different. Children have personalities; treat them as such. They desire respect, understanding, and hearing. Give them choices: Don't compel your kids to do what you want. Give them alternatives, such as a storybook, video game, or cloud presence.

Children desire your attention, presence, and participation in their activities. So, give your kids time. Books are the source of knowledge. Encourage reading. When they're reading, read with them. Reading aloud to youngsters encourages them to read. You read your youngster a paragraph. Parents are loved by their children.

Reading builds community. Interaction is crucial to emotional growth. You must ask many questions and answer your child's. Interactive toys can amuse and educate youngsters. Blocks help kids learn the alphabet and numbers. Children don't enjoy seriousness. Thus, they prefer cartoons over literature—plan playtime. Tell them to play after breakfast. Seeing is believing. Take them to the zoo instead of explaining or watching a tiger movie. Try out routines.

Co-parent: Both parents must care for their kids. This is crucial for a child's mental health. Fathers should be involved, too. Dads are seldom engaged in parenting. They don't feed or clean them. Research shows that dad-cared kids succeed in school and acquire problem-solving abilities. Most mothers are always with their kids.

Children may get bored. Moms should design kid-friendly activities. You have fond childhood recollections, right? Remember when your day read your stories? Remember playing board games with your mom? Make activities: Children often get bored. They no longer like the toy they liked last week. Make activities. Children may find washing a dog or watering plants entertaining.

Children are picky eaters, so master the kitchen. Mothers struggle with feeding their children. Always test different recipes. Let them cook: Children like cooking. Children love cooking with their parents. Don't allow children to play with knives or near the stove; they may whip eggs, sort veggies, and set the table. Children adore muck and water, so try gardening.

Help kids spread seeds, water plants, and explore nature in the garden. Children adore *pets and birds. Your kids will love a dog, cat, parrot, or fish. Children prefer real animals over toy automobiles. When you confess your faults, your children will learn to apologise. Admitting errors to your kid won't change you. Nature can teach your kid many things. Tell your youngster how trees aid humans and how humans rely on the environment and the surrounding topography. Tell your youngster how the environment affects humans to teach them environmental care.*

Teach kids to reuse, not squander. Tell him why water is vital and not to waste it. Encourage social responsibility by making garbage picking a game.

Teach kindness: Encourage your child's compassion. Encourage compassion towards the homeless, animals, and destitute. What type of kid will you raise if you lie? Always tell the truth if you want your youngster to behave. By telling the truth, you'll attract a decent person. If you repeatedly lie to your children, they will stop believing you. Your youngster won't respect or adore you if you lie. White falsehoods are nonetheless harmful.

Attend PTMs, school functions, and Always school get-togethers. Kids adore it when mom and dad go to school together. Don't nag your partner: Children from fighting homes tend to be feeble. Partner arguments are frequent. Argue while the kids aren't around. Praise in public, condemn privately. Your husband and kids should get it too. Remember! Respect your partner In homes where women respect their males and vice versa, children respect their parents.

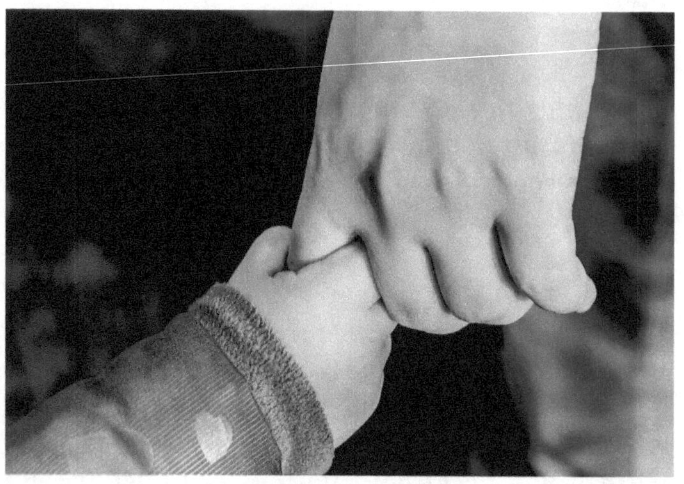

Your kid will love his parents more if you respect them. Respect parenting differences. Your partner's parenting philosophy may vary from yours. Your spouse's parenting technique isn't harmful to the kid. Therefore, encourage it.

Praise your child: Praising your kid is essential. He'll perform better when praised. Even if he's not good, commend him for trying. Children require good feedback. She'll feel worse if you call her drawing bad. Instead of declaring the picture is poor, suggest, "Erase this line and draw another curve here." Acknowledge and celebrate the children's efforts and successes. Recognize, affirm, and instil pride in the recipient. Emphasize advancing and expanding. Assist them in finding an appropriate educational fit.

Avoid negative feedback. Negative feedback deters children. Negative comments may

discourage a youngster from trying again. Even if your kid gets an "E," don't criticise him. Rewarding youngsters has a positive influence on their psyche. Reward your child's success. You may promise him a bike if he earns an "A" on his next test.

Cherish his achievements: If your youngster gets high marks, praise him. Put your child's racing trophy among your valuables. Attend any competitions your youngster enters. Embrace him if he survives. If he fails, applaud his effort.

Your kid is precious to you, but does he realise it? Always make your youngster feel unique. It's better to gossip about your kid to dad than in front of him. You know your kid best, so trust your instincts. Even if you're incorrect, you're probably right. Know when to say yes and no while disciplining a youngster.

Say NO when your youngster is suspicious and intolerant: Don't allow your child to be rude to you or others. Stop his intolerance. Praise and rewards may boost your child's confidence. Participating in a child's activities helps inspire confidence. If your youngster is furious, distract him with fun activities. Hug a weeping youngster to reassure him.

Teach your kids EMPATHY by narrating moral tales from your youth. Encourage children to see things from the points of view of a variety of different people and groups. This involves respecting people's diversity in terms of their colour, religion, sexual orientation, age, sentiments, skill levels, and other aspects of their identities.

Use technology to meet your children's needs. Teach your youngster what's ethical and immoral. Help him grasp ethics. Morality distinguishes good from evil and refers to *appropriate action. Raise a morally responsible child through teaching morals. Tell them the worth of values.*

Tell your youngster why being kind and honest necessary. Food fights are prevalent, so avoid them. If your youngster won't eat a specific meal, offer another or inquire what he likes. Suppose he won't eat, fine. He won't starve.

Parenting is exhausting; make a timetable. A timetable may simplify your job—schedule tasks. Encourage your kids to sing, dance, write, draw, and play instruments. Creativity boosts cerebral ability. Research reveals physical exercise boosts brain growth. Encourage walking, running, and outdoor play.

Get your youngster all the needed immunizations. Regular medical visits are also important. Ignore health complaints. Encourage your youngster to clean teeth, wash hands and feet, and take baths. Learning should become a habit.

Never leave newborns and toddlers alone. When riding a bike or scooter, he should wear a helmet.

Reconsider medication administration Avoid antibiotics whenever possible. Promote independence: Overdependence on you will hamper your child's growth. Tell him you're constantly with him, yet send him alone.

Expect the best. Expect great things from your kid, but don't push him too far. Let your youngster try: Don't do what your youngster can do. Not allowing your kid to eat alone is hurting his learning process. Unless it's essential, don't redo your child's work. Your youngster won't want to do it alone. How do you help your youngster reach a toy on a high shelf? Stop buying her stuff.

Assign a task Encourage your youngster to separate coloured clothing for washing, pick up books, and pick up garden litter. Create a routine: Your youngster should read, do homework, play games, and watch TV regularly. Let them help plan your day. Develop predictable routines:

Children learn rapidly with a daily routine. The practice should include cleaning teeth before night, washing hands before meals, and praying daily. Encourage collaboration: Humans are social creatures, and cooperation is the key to success.

Teach your youngster to get along with others. Children are skilled at throwing tantrums. Teaching etiquette helps control outbursts. Teach them good manners.

Make rules and enforce them. Children's rules might vary from "don't litter" to "don't speak to strangers." Sometimes you must make expressions or dress goofy to make your youngster giggle. Teach your youngster when to quit watching TV, playing video games, and going to bed. Use infographics to educate your child: Research shows that infographics and visuals help kids learn more quickly.

Give children picture books to help them comprehend things. Children learn more quickly when they watch instructive films.

Use kid-friendly language If your youngster finishes schoolwork, take them to the park. Finish your schoolwork, we'll go to the park.

Reactions varied. No profanity! Never swear in front of a youngster. No "crap" or "idiot." Inform them about CHILD ABUSE indicators.

Comparing your kid to another can cause jealousy and hostility. Everyone needs amusement, right? Take your youngster to a movie or watch one at home. Playing music will relax you and your youngster. What if kids dispute over the same toy? Encourage collaboration. One youngster may play for 10 minutes, then another.

Let your youngster resolve his quarrel until one of them becomes aggressive. Let kids resolve their conflicts. Learn to distract your youngster. Bring chart paper if your youngster is sketching on the wall.

Manage meltdowns: Your youngster may resist going to school. Give him your photo or a heart-shaped tissue to show you care. When your kid shreds papers and throws them on the floor, instruct him to gather them and dump them in the trash. Say "Sorry" and "Thank you" often. If your youngster acts wrong, admonish them quickly. Do it now. Children are proactive and require sleep. According to research, one hour of sleep loss reduces sixth-IQ graders to that of a fourth-grader.

Honesty is the best policy. Research shows that an honest youngster will become a responsible adult. Your youngster may lie to please or get rewards. Always verify a child's story. You need rules, just like kids. Setting rules for kids means following your own. If you don't want your youngster to watch late-night TV, don't either.

Too much control leads to drug use, drinking, and smoking. Never do it before them! If you're too busy, your youngster may be bored. When bored, kids turn to smoking, drinking, and drugs. Moderate arguing benefits youngsters, research shows. Teaching gratitude is an excellent trait. Your kids must be grateful.

Create a child-friendly setting. Parenthood involves creating the correct environment. Happiness, love, compassion, and discipline are needed. The kid's strengths and weaknesses should be taken into account while developing reasonable expectations for the youngster. It is preferable to provide children with alternatives, to take a flexible approach to completing jobs that include a variety of possibilities, and to be receptive to the children's ever-evolving needs, interests, and concerns.

You intended to be a doctor but became a marketer. Don't push your youngster to achieve your goals.

Know the child's requirements Your kid is your business's heir. Reasonable. Does your kid want to emulate you?

You should make your youngster feel special, but don't pamper them. Too much boasting about your kid spoils him. As a parent, you're your child's first teacher. Your kid can teach you a lot. Having a kid makes you more teachable.

Be happy: Becoming a parent was your decision. What will the youngster learn through your stress, rage, fear, worry, and jealousy? Toddlers have tantrums, adolescents are defiant. You can't fix children's behavioural issues unless you know their desires. Communicate to solve problems.

Keep the kids occupied to keep them calm. Find out what entertains your youngster the most. Children become bored with everyday living, so they take trips to spice things up. This strengthens bonds.

Organize children's parties to express how much you adore him. Invite his pals. Children and parents benefit from parties because they stimulate social engagement. Check the development process. Observe your children's body changes.

Before they learn from the outside world, teach them about personality, character, and SEX

EDUCATION.

Verify learning: Check your child's progress. Check his notebooks, reports, and assignments. Never assign homework. Watch them studying. Bullying may harm a child's mental development.

Determine whether your kid is bullied at home or school. Children as young as 5 use the internet; thus, checking for cyberbullying is essential. Identify cyberbullying. Check your kids' internet activity. The Internet provides information. The Internet has many unpleasant aspects, too. Know their IDs and passwords.

Good parents are their kids' Facebook friends. TV is a source of learning and fun; use parental controls. TV may hurt children, though. It is important to provide children with honest feedback on who they are. For example, if children misbehave or act out, you should work with them to understand the implications or effects of their actions (both on themselves and on others), and you should also model other types of conduct for them. Be constructive. It is possible for parents to react to unacceptable conduct in their kid without scolding the youngster.

Use parental controls online. Block harmful sites to prevent youngsters from visiting porn and unlawful sites. Children will always confide in friends over parents. Their pals aren't the finest advisors. Childhood buddies may confide in you. Let them select a career: Your kids' needs come first.

Your best may not be their best. Advise, but let them choose. When your kids need you, be there. One misstep may ruin them. Parents come first, then kids.

Don't make your child's life easy. Parents have it tough, too. Money is necessary, so teach its worth. Teach kids that making money is hard. Check how they're spending pocket money. If kids discover how hard it is to create money, they'll spend less and save more.

Happy families aren't accidental. They're raised deliberately. Make family meals and family fun time journeys a priority. Encourage youngsters to cherish their connections with caring people who can provide them assistance and to make use of such connections. Members of one's own family, instructors, coaches, mentors, or friends who are able to provide direction and confidence may fall into this category. The power that comes from working together and being part of a community.

One day, your adolescent will be ready to leave home (for work, education etc.). Your kid is your child at 1 or 50. Don't sacrifice your health: Your children are your lifeblood, but you should never sacrifice your health.

One of the biggest causes of conflict between parents and children is parental ownership. Parents assume kids enjoy pets. Free their LIVING.

Get help: Parenting isn't easy. Everyone's parenting style is different. Join a parenting group if you're experiencing trouble.

Raise a giver: There is so much pleasure in giving. Teach your child to become a giver. Let your child understand the importance of giving. Remember, YOU just can not raise as you were raised!

Don't let them get away with meanness: Children can be very mean. They are likely to do emotional blackmailing. Be involved in their lives. Resilience may drive forward progress.

Assist youngsters in developing the skills necessary to face and prevail over adversity and uncertainty by assisting them in conceiving of and putting into action novel and concerted methods that make challenging circumstances bearable and in achieving success in conquering obstacles.

Ask your kids to help you: When you need extra hands for household work, ask your children to volunteer. This will make your children respond to the family's needs. Frequently ask them to do Car Wash or water the plants together.

Don't yell: Generally speaking, yelling will produce a parent-deaf kid. This shall also cause a dislike with either of the parents by the kid for life.

Move close, but give them privacy: You need to be close to your kids and provide them with privacy. Know their friends and observe their routines. Never bridge their interest but feed their likes.

Happy Parenting, Guys!

Cheers!!

www.authordheerajmehrotra.com

About The Author

Dheeraj Mehrotra, MS, MPhil, PhD (Education Management) honoris causa., a white and a yellow belt in SIX SIGMA, a Certified NLP Business Diploma holder, is an Educational Innovator, Author, with expertise in Six Sigma In Education, Academic Audits, Neuro-Linguistic Programming (NLP), Total Quality Management In Education, an Experiential Educator, a CBSE Resource towards School Assessment (SQAA), CCE, JIT, Five S, and

KAIZEN. He has authored over 100 books on topics which include Computer Science, AI, Digital Body Language, NLP, Quality Circles, School Management, Classroom Effectiveness and Safety and security in schools.

A former Principal at De Indian Public School, New Delhi, (INDIA), NPS International School, Guwahati, and Education Officer at GEMS, Gurgaon, with an ample teaching experience of over Two Decades, he is a certified Trainer for Quality Circles/ TQM in Education and QCI Standards for School Accreditation/ School Audits and Management. He has also been honoured with the President of India's National Teacher Award in the year 2006 and the Best Science Teacher State Award (By the Ministry of Science and Technology, State of UP), Innovation in Education for his inception of Six Sigma In Education by Education Watch, New Delhi and Education World- Best Teacher Award, BOLT Learner Teacher Award by Air India, 'Innovation in Education Award 2016' by Higher Education Forum (HEF), Gujarat Chapter, among others. He has developed over 150 FREE EDUCATIONAL MOBILE Apps for the Google Play Store exclusively for Teachers, Students, and Parents. This work has been recognised by the LIMCA BOOK OF RECORDS & INDIA BOOK OF RECORDS as the only Indian to draw that feast. Dr Mehrotra works as a PRINCIPAL at KUNWARS GLOBAL SCHOOL, Lucknow, in India. He has conducted over 1000 workshops globally on "Excellence In Education" integrated with Total Quality Management and Six Sigma, Technology Integration in Education (TIE), Developing towards being ROCKSTAR TEACHERS, including Cyberspace, Cyber Security, Classroom Management, School Leadership & Management, and Innovative teaching within classrooms via Mind Maps, NLP and Experiential Learning in

Academics. He is an active TEDx speaker and can be viewed on the youtube TEDx channel.

As a premium UDEMY Instructor, he has developed over 450 courses and caters to over 8 Lakh students from 180 countries.

He can be visited at www.authordheerajmehrotra.com.

BY NATIONAL
AWARDEE
EDUCATOR
Kindle Price: ₹ 72.00
inclusive of all taxes
Teaching
in the
VUCA
WORLD
Dr. Dheeraj Mehrotra
authordheerajmehrotra.com
Flipkart
available at
amazon

Child
Safeguarding
in
Schools
Dr Dheeraj
Mehrotra